Letts

Framework FOCUS

Red Hot
ICT
Starters

David Sadler
Max Begley

Contents

iii

Acknowledgements

We would like to thank our colleagues at Amery Hill School and Frogmore Community College for their support before and during the writing of this book. Thanks to Rachel Sadler for her help, especially in getting started. Her experience of writing starters for English was invaluable.

Thanks are also due to others who have supported us at previous schools and the Hampshire inspectors for their encouragement and for recommending the book for use in all Hampshire schools.

Introduction

Introducing starters

As endorsed by the Key Stage 3 Framework for teaching ICT, lessons are now taught in three parts. They should begin with a 10–15 minute starter, followed by the main part of the lesson and finally a plenary. The starter can occur in many forms, from a written activity to a role-play, with students working in groups, pairs or individually. This will depend on the size of your class and what you feel most comfortable with.

Target audience

This book is suitable for teachers of Key Stage 3 ICT, however the ideas and approach can be used at Key Stage 2, 4 and at post 16. The book will also be a useful tool for anyone entering the profession or transferring to teach ICT.

Timing of starters

The starters in this book are flexible; they can take as little as 10 minutes, if you feel that this is enough time to get your point across. However, you can use a longer session if you feel your students will benefit from further practice.

It is often beneficial to choose a starter related to the main objective of the lesson, because this focuses the students' minds ready for the task to come. Alternatively, starters can act as a reminder or revision tool.

You may find that the activities in some starters are useful as plenary activities to test students' understanding at the end of a lesson or topic. This is a particularly good idea for the more noisy and physical starters.

Due to the nature of the subject, there is no need to have a starter every lesson but certainly one or two during a topic will provoke interest and help cement knowledge.

How to use this book

Contents grid

For simplicity, each starter has been assigned to one specific year group and one objective. However, all the activities are extremely flexible. Most of them can be used for any Key Stage 3 year group and adapted according to your students' abilities.

Objectives and aims

Each starter activity has been matched to an appropriate Key Stage 3 Framework objective and subsequent task related aim. A number of the objectives are very complex and cannot be fully covered by a starter activity. Where this happens, the starter focuses on an essential part of the objective.

Resources

The activities are designed to require as little preparation as possible, with little need to photocopy additional material. Where preparation is necessary, this will either be preparing files in shared areas or preparing worksheets/cards for pupils to hold up.

Activities

The instructions for each activity are presented as short, bulleted action points, to minimise the time required for planning.

Answers

Answers, where needed, are provided on the same page as the questions to save valuable time spent leafing through the back pages. Several of the activities have numerous alternative answers, which leads to healthy class discussion.

Differentiation

The up arrow ⇑ represents more challenging activities, whereas the down arrow ⇓ represents an easier version. However, some of the suggestions are really alternative versions of the activity, rather than being significantly harder or easier. Many of these ideas can be further adapted and can be used as a basis to inspire even more creative lessons.

Many teachers have a selection of great starter activities that they know work in the classroom. However, what many of us are lacking is a quick, portable reference book that we can use to refresh our memories and inspire ourselves from time to time.

We feel that we have written so much material over the past few years that gets put in a filing cabinet, forgotten and never used again that a resource like this book will be of great help to us and hopefully to you.

David Sadler and Max Begley

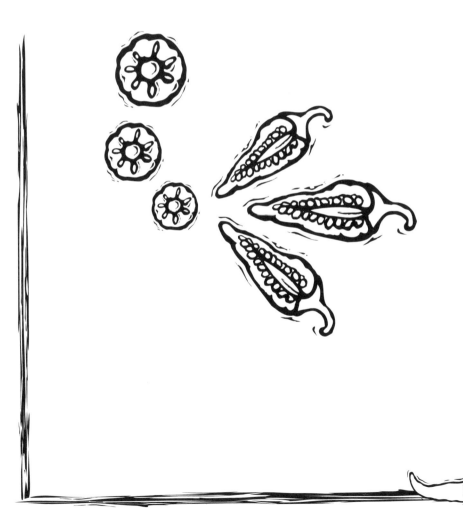

Watch out

Objective covered

F1 *Understand that different forms of information – text, graphics, sound, numeric data and symbols – can be combined to create meaning and impact.*

Aim

To know that there are different ways to present information and understand when they are used.

Activity

⊛ Ask the students to brainstorm different types of warning. Make a list on the board. Ideas may include speed bumps, hand signals, road signs, yellow cards, departure signs in airports and alarms.

⊛ Discuss why each warning is presented in that way, for example foghorns use sound because the danger may not be visible.

⊛ Finish with questions to the class, asking how they would warn people about:

- a hurricane
- power being cut temporarily
- driving the wrong way down a one-way street.

Differentiation

⊛ ⇓ Only use two or three very different warnings, for example speed bumps, alarms and yellow cards.

1

Sell, sell, sell

Objective covered

F2 *Identify the purpose of an information source (e.g. to present facts or opinions, to advertise, publicise or entertain) and whether it is likely to be biased.*

Aim

To be able to identify whether the text is informative, persuasive or to entertain.

Resources

An advert.
The front page of a newspaper.
The first page of a novel.

Activity

⊛ Display the different types of text.

⊛ Discuss with the class the aim of each article/text and what they are trying to achieve, for example: advert for a child's toy – persuasive text – selling to children.

Differentiation

⊛ ⇑ Get the students to think of other examples of text and to identify what the text is trying to achieve in the same way.

⊛ ⇓ Use a smaller amount of less complex text and read through it with the class as you discuss it.

Going away

Objective covered
F3 *Identify what information is relevant to a task.*

Aim
To be able to identify what information
is needed to plan a holiday.

Activity
⊛ Organise the class into pairs. Ask them to list things they
would need to know before booking a holiday.

⊛ List one item from each pair on the board. Discuss where
you might find each piece of information.

Differentiation
⊛ ⇑ Discuss which pieces of information would be needed first.
Order the items on the board.

⊛ ⇓ Use a less complex task, for example a trip to the cinema.

You are a winner

Objective covered
F4 *Understand how someone using an information source could be misled by missing or inaccurate information.*

Aim
To understand that information can have a hidden agenda.

Activity
⊛ Display a screen-shot from an Internet advert (or write something similar on the board), for example:

> YOU ARE A WINNER! <u>CLICK HERE</u> TO CLAIM YOUR PRIZE

⊛ Ask the class if they have seen this sort of advert. Ask how many have actually won. Ask whether they claimed their prize – was it worth it?

⊛ Discuss with the class what is normally in the small print.

⊛ Ask the students to write down what the small print might be for this advert. Ask them what the company is trying to achieve.

Answers
Any suitable examples, such as: calls cost £1 per minute, minimum call time 45 minutes, prize may be shared between a large number of winners.

Differentiation
⊛ ⇑ Discuss the purpose of supermarket loyalty cards and what the supermarkets are trying to achieve.

⊛ ⇑ Ask the students to design an Internet advert to sell CD players. They should include different screens and the small print.

That's a fact

Objective covered

F1a *Understand how the content and style of an information source affect its suitability for particular purposes, by considering its mix of fact, opinion and material designed to advertise, publicise or entertain.*

Aim

To be able to identify fact and opinion in a newspaper article.

Resources

Several copies of a sports report from a newspaper.
Highlighter pens in two colours.

Activity

- ❀ Discuss with the class the meaning of 'fact' and 'opinion' with suitable examples, such as 'Talika is 12. He is a good boy.'

- ❀ Distribute a sports report from a newspaper. Ask the class to highlight facts and opinions in different colours.

- ❀ Go through the article and check that there is agreement.

Differentiation

- ❀ ⇑ Use a political or more complex article.

- ❀ ⇓ Use pre-prepared text, or a simple tabloid article.

5

A sporting audience

Objective covered

F1c *Understand how the content and style of an information source affect its suitability for particular purposes, by considering the clarity, accessibility and plausibility of the material.*

Aim

To understand how the same material can be adapted for different audiences.

Resources

Several copies of two reports of the same sporting event, one from a tabloid paper, the other from a broadsheet.

Activity

- ⊛ In pairs or as individuals, ask the students to list five differences between the articles.

- ⊛ Collect the differences from the class, listing them on the board.

- ⊛ Ask the students why they think the different types of newspaper write their articles differently.

Differentiation

⊛ ⇓ Use articles with fewer words and more images.

Weather it's good enough

Objective covered

F2 *Devise and apply criteria to evaluate how well various information sources will support a task.*

Aim

To be able to evaluate two different weather websites.

Resources

Computers with Internet access.

Activity

⊛ Ask the class to brainstorm ten things that they think would make a good weather website. List these on the board.

⊛ Organise the students into small groups. Ask them to decide which five factors are most important.

⊛ The students should then go on to the Internet and look at two sites (www.bbc.co.uk/weather and www.metoffice.com) and decide which is better for the five factors they have chosen.

⊛ As a class, the students should then decide which is the best overall site and why.

Answers

Ideas might include: good maps, clear symbols, wind symbols, temperature symbols, colour mix, fast loading, regional and world forecasts, simple words, user friendly, includes a summary, long-term forecasts and good animations.

Differentiation

⊛ ⇓ Compare two different information sources using the same criteria, for example a newspaper article and website.

Paper, online or CD?

Objective covered

F3 *Justify the use of particular information sources to support an investigation or presentation.*

Aim

To understand the advantages and disadvantages of information in different forms.

Resources

Examples of information on CD-ROM and in an encyclopedia.

Activity

⊛ Show the students examples of information from a CD-ROM and an encyclopedia.

⊛ Get the class to brainstorm advantages and disadvantages of each.

Answers

Discussion should include audio clips, films and moving images, transfer of information (copy and paste), size, adaptability of text, accessibility, computer crash problems and the need for a printer.

Differentiation

⊛ ⇑ Ask the students to think of other software that appears in different forms and discuss the advantages and disadvantages of each. Examples could include atlases, 3-D fly throughs (see Ordnance Survey site, www.ordsvy.gov.uk) and animated explanations (www.howstuffworks.com).

⊛ ⇓ Choose obvious examples from the CD-ROM (ones with animation or video).

Where, who, what and why?

Objective covered

F1a *Select information sources and data systematically for an identified purpose by judging the reliability of the information sources.*

Aim

To evaluate two different presentations of the same information for different audiences.

Activity

- Split the class into small groups.

- Write these subjects on the board: last night's football scores, the top ten singles, the latest news headlines, a news story from six months ago, the latest cricket score, information on a tourist destination.

- In their groups, the students should discuss where the best place would be to find information on two of these subjects.

- They need to nominate a speaker who will report back to the class explaining where they would look for the information and why.

Answers

Prompt students to think about the Internet, newspapers, TV, radio, Teletext, books, magazines and so on.

Differentiation

- ⇩ The students should discuss fewer topics. You could perhaps choose topics directed to what might interest them.

You're biased

Objective covered

F1b *Select information sources and data systematically for an identified purpose by identifying possible bias due to sampling methods.*

Aim

To understand what bias is and how it can mislead people.

Activity

- ✸ Write on the board a type of incident that could be written about in a newspaper, for example a football match.

- ✸ Get the students to write a paragraph from three points of view: one from each side of the argument and a neutral one. For example, one player or manager from each team and the referee.

- ✸ Read out one article from each point of view and highlight the differences.

Differentiation

- ✸ ⇑ Use a more complex incident.

- ✸ ⇓ Divide the students into small groups and allocate each group one point of view.

Questionnaire or tally?

Objective covered

F1c *Select information and data systematically for an identified purpose by collecting valid, accurate data efficiently.*

Aim

To be able to collect data to get specific results.

Activity

⊛ Tell the students that when you carry out a survey, you can ask people to fill in a questionnaire themselves or you can add a tally to a tally chart to record their response. Explain the difference between closed and open questions – closed questions have a choice of answers, open questions could have any answer.

⊛ Split the class into two, and tell them they are going to carry out a survey to find out about TV viewing habits. Ask one half to think of closed questions, with responses that could be recorded using a tally chart. Ask the other half to think of open questions for a questionnaire that respondents fill in themselves.

⊛ Compare a good example of each type of survey and get the students to predict why the results would be different by asking questions in these different ways.

Differentiation

⊛ ⇑ Ask how the design of the questionnaire might affect the results.

⊛ ⇓ Give them examples of a questionnaire and tally chart and ask them to compare these in the same way.

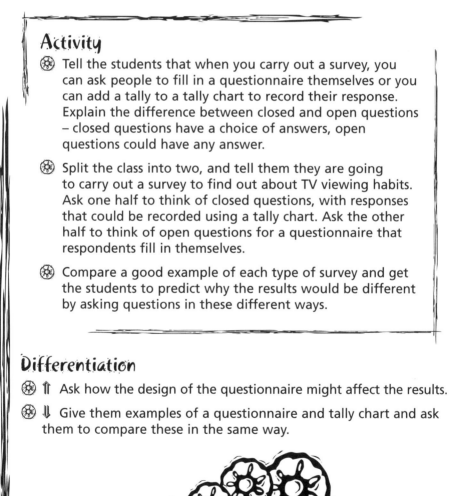

Hands up, it's the law

Objective covered
F1d *Select information sources and data systematically for an identified purpose by recognising potential misuse of collected data.*

Aim
To be able to identify whether an issue involves the Data Protection Act, Computer Misuse Act, Health and Safety, or Copyright and Patents.

Resources
Several sets of these cards:

DATA PROTECTION ACT	COMPUTER MISUSE ACT
HEALTH AND SAFETY	COPYRIGHT©

Activity

⊛ Split the class into small groups or pairs (ideally fours). Give each group a set of cards.

⊛ Read out the following scenarios, getting each group to hold up the relevant card. Give answers before moving on.

1   Sending a virus

2   Dentist asking for a credit card number on registering

3   Using someone else's username and password

4   Leaving computer cables trailing across a room

5   Using software registered to someone else

6   Getting RSI in the wrist due to bad keyboard position

7   Keeping information on a database for a long time without updating it

8   Copying a CD and selling it to a friend

Answers
1 CMA   2 DPA   3 CMA   4 H&S   5 ©   6 H&S   7 DPA   8 ©

First to find

Objective covered

F5 *Search a variety of sources for information relevant to a task (e.g. using indexes, search techniques, navigational structures and engines).*

Aim

To understand how to use a keyword search to find specific pieces of information.

Resources

Computers with Internet access.

Activity

- Demonstrate how to use a search engine such as www.google.co.uk or www.yahoo.co.uk to find a football club website.

- Write five questions on the board such as:

    1 Who is the goalkeeper for Frome Town FC?

    2 Who invented Barbie?

    3 How much does a CO_2 fire extinguisher cost?

    4 How old was Elvis Presley when he died?

    5 What is the capital city of Mauritius?

- Ask the students to put their hands up when they find each answer. The first student to raise their hand should tell the class how they found the answer.

Differentiation

- ⇩ Either give questions on cards aimed at each student's ability or give fewer questions with simpler solutions.

Reducing the hits

Objective covered

F6 *Narrow down a search to achieve more relevant results.*

Aim

To be able to reduce the amount of unwanted or irrelevant websites in a search.

Resources

Computers with Internet access.

Activity

⊛ Explain to the students that you want to find sites on Cheddar cheese.

⊛ Tell the students to type in *cheddar* at a search engine. Ask them to tell you how many hits they get. Explain that they can be more specific by typing *"cheddar cheese"* as the speech marks make the search engine look for those words in that order.

⊛ Tell the class that Cheddar is not only famous for cheese. The students can reduce the number of hits further by typing *"cheddar cheese" -gorge -caves*. Ask them to tell you how many hits there are now.

Differentiation

⊛ ⇑ Ask the students to reduce the number of hits without prompting.

⊛ ⇑ Get them to use other words to reduce the number of hits further, for example *"official site"*.

⊛ ⇓ Use a very basic search, for example *"Bristol City"*, and compare to *"Bristol City Football Club"*. Then try *"Bristol City" -council*.

Which image?

Objective covered
F7 *Assess the value of information from various sources to a particular task.*

Aim
To be able to choose a relevant picture for the purpose.

Resources
OHP or worksheet with different images on, for example:
1 Letterhead for a fitness centre.

2 Advert for a golf course.

Activity
- Get the students to choose which image is appropriate for each purpose.
- Discuss with the class which they would use and why.

Differentiation
- ⬆ The discussion should involve target audience, purpose and design.
- ⬇ Choose a purpose with three very simple images with a more obvious answer.

Finding it again

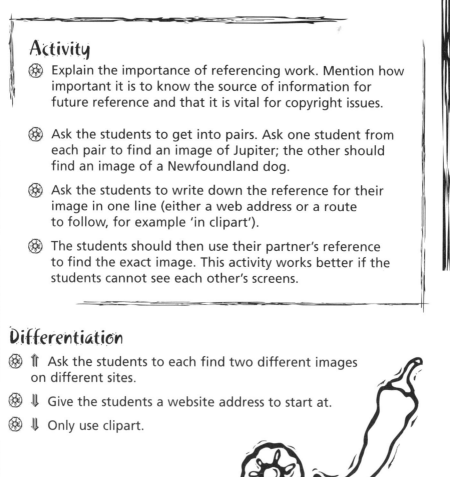

YEAR 7

Objective covered
F8 *Acknowledge sources of information used.*

Aim
To be able to reference work so that it is easy to retrace your steps.

Resources
Computers with Internet access.

Activity
⊛ Explain the importance of referencing work. Mention how important it is to know the source of information for future reference and that it is vital for copyright issues.

⊛ Ask the students to get into pairs. Ask one student from each pair to find an image of Jupiter; the other should find an image of a Newfoundland dog.

⊛ Ask the students to write down the reference for their image in one line (either a web address or a route to follow, for example 'in clipart').

⊛ The students should then use their partner's reference to find the exact image. This activity works better if the students cannot see each other's screens.

Differentiation
⊛ ⇧ Ask the students to each find two different images on different sites.

⊛ ⇩ Give the students a website address to start at.

⊛ ⇩ Only use clipart.

16

+, - or " "

Objective covered

F4 *Extend and refine search methods to be more efficient (e.g. using synonyms and AND, OR, NOT).*

Aim

To be able to find a specific piece of information using multiple search criteria.

Resources

Computers with Internet access.

Activity

✳ Using www.google.co.uk, demonstrate to the students what each of the symbols +, - and "" mean by searching for *"youth hostels" +children -england*. This will find websites that have information on youth hostels that take children, but are not in England.

✳ Ask the students to find the telephone number for the local leisure centre in a similar way. They must use symbols, for example *"Alton Sports Centre" +hampshire -derbyshire*.

Differentiation

✳ ⇑ Ask the students to try two or three more complex searches, for example to find a local garage that sells a particular make of car.

✳ ⇓ Ask the students to do the same activity using more user-friendly websites such as www.scoot.co.uk or www.yell.com.

Best place to look

Objective covered

F5 *Explain the advantages of the methods used by different search engines and programs to search for data in various formats.*

Aim

To understand the difference between a search engine and a web directory and what makes a good example of each.

Resources

Computers with Internet access.

Activity

⊛ Explain that a search engine is a program that looks for keywords and phrases and produces a list of sites including that word. Explain that a web directory is a list of categorised sites sorted by humans.

⊛ Demonstrate a simple search on a search engine such as www.ask.co.uk or www.google.co.uk. Then use a web directory such as www.yahoo.co.uk. Emphasise the problems and good points of each and discuss with the class.

⊛ Ask the students to rate the different search engines and web directories.

Answers

Some suggestions:
Altavista – massive, but not many educational sites.
Excite – great at general searches, but not so good for a specific search.
Infoseek – small, but lots of educational sites.
Google – one of the better search engines, it actually searches other search engines!
Yahoo – very user friendly, well categorised sites.
Ask – easy to use, but hard to find anything. Often answers the wrong question.

Differentiation

⊛ ⇓ Only ask the students to rate one directory and one search engine.

How do you get to school?

Objective covered

F2a *As part of a study, analyse high-volume quantitative and qualitative data systematically by exploring the data to form and test hypotheses.*

Aim

To be able to predict current trends in transport to school by analysing past information.

Resources

Pie charts showing how students travelled to school in 1914 and 1960.

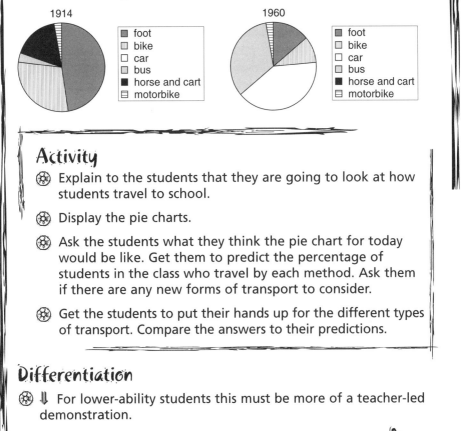

1914

■	foot
▦	bike
□	car
▨	bus
■	horse and cart
☰	motorbike

1960

■	foot
▦	bike
□	car
▨	bus
■	horse and cart
☰	motorbike

Activity

- ✦ Explain to the students that they are going to look at how students travel to school.

- ✦ Display the pie charts.

- ✦ Ask the students what they think the pie chart for today would be like. Get them to predict the percentage of students in the class who travel by each method. Ask them if there are any new forms of transport to consider.

- ✦ Get the students to put their hands up for the different types of transport. Compare the answers to their predictions.

Differentiation

✦ ⬇ For lower-ability students this must be more of a teacher-led demonstration.

Perfectly proportioned

Objective covered

F2b *As part of a study, analyse high-volume quantitative and qualitative data systematically by identifying correlations between variables.*

Aim

To be able to spot whether there is a relationship between hand size and foot size.

Resources

OHP or board prepared with the following data in a table and as a line graph or scatter graph.

Name	Hand size (cm)	Foot size
John	8	7
Jane	6	4
Michael	10	12
Michelle	6	5
Carl	9	10
Carla	7	5

Activity

✻ Ask the students if they spot a relationship between hand and foot size – can they work out what it is?

Differentiation

✻ ⇑ Focus more on working out what the relationship is and less on spotting it.

✻ ⇓ Ask the students why they think there is a relationship. (If you're bigger, you're bigger all over.)

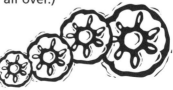

Predicting the future

Objective covered

F2c *As part of a study, analyse high-volume quantitative and qualitative data systematically by drawing valid conclusions and making predictions.*

Aim

To be able to collect data to get specific results.

Resources

Pie charts showing how students travelled to school in 1914, 1960 and today (see 'How do you get to school?', page 19).

Activity

- Ask the students to think about what we can learn from the pie charts. For example, increase in the use of motorised transport, decrease in the number of students who make their own way to school, more students go to school together.

- Ask them to predict how students will travel to school in 30 years time. Will the proportions change? Will there be any new forms of transport?

- Ask them if they think this pattern will occur in all areas of the country. What regional differences are there? Can the assumption be applied to all schools? Prompt them to think about comparing rural and urban areas.

Differentiation

- ⇑ Focus more on the reasons why there are differences and why changes have occurred.

- ⇓ Concentrate on the forms of transport.

Product database

Objective covered

F9a *In an investigation, design and use an appropriate data handling structure to answer questions and draw conclusions.*

Aim

To know what information is needed about a product for a shop or warehouse database.

Activity

✽ Explain that bar codes are used in shops to recognise an item. Once recognised, the computer can give all the information.

✽ Ask the students what information they think is needed for this system to work.

✽ Write their answers on the board in a list down the side.

✽ Using appropriate questions, lead the students to the field type needed for each field. Examples are: product name (text), price (currency), sell-by date (date/time), supplier (text), weight (numeric).

Differentiation

✽ ⇑ Ask the students to prioritise the information and design the layout for a database form.

✽ ⇓ Use a product as an example, such as cornflakes.

Open or closed?

Objective covered

F9b *In an investigation, design a questionnaire or data collection sheet to provide relevant data.*

Aim

To know how to create a questionnaire to collect meaningful data.

Activity

⊛ Ask students individually to think of five fields that they would need to put into an address book.

⊛ Remind the class of the difference between open and closed questions. Give examples such as *Title: Mr/Mrs/Ms/Miss/other* (closed) and *Name:* (open). Get them to decide which questions need to be open and which can be closed.

⊛ Ask the students to design a questionnaire on paper.

Answers

Examples of closed questions are gender, star sign and age. Examples of open questions are address and occupation.

Differentiation

⊛ ⇑ Ask the students to think of more questions.

⊛ ⇓ Get the students to design the questionnaire on a computer.

⊛ ⇓ Give the students the questions and ask them to decide whether they are open or closed.

Check your work

Objective covered
F9c *In an investigation, check data efficiently for errors.*

Aim
To be able to check information for errors.

Resources
Worksheets showing a table like this one:

CUSTOMER INFORMATION DATABASE				
Name	Address	Postcode	Age	Phone number
John	18 Barrel Rd	GU34 6GG	23	07893 555555
Smith	1 Sipton St	SO23 8HH	167	07423 444444
Brown	4 Random Rd	B45THTY	forty	654 333333
Johnson	Bradford	D34 6TT	28	0665 222222

Activity
⊛ Explain to the class that verification is the process of checking data on a computer after they have been input to make sure they are correct.

⊛ Hand out the worksheets. Ask students to highlight any information that seems incorrect by underlining it.

Answers
John, 167, B45THTY, forty, 654 333333, Bradford

Differentiation
⊛ ⇑ Discuss how data could be validated (checked on entry by the computer) to reduce the need for verification.

Which graph?

Objective covered

F9e *In an investigation, use software to represent data in simple graphs, charts or tables, justifying the choice of representation.*

Aim

To know when it is appropriate to use different types of graph.

Resources

Sets of cards showing different types of graphs similar to the ones below:

Activity

⊛ Give each student a set of cards.

⊛ Explain that you are going to read out information you might see on a graph. Ask them to hold up the card showing the graph they would use to display it.

⊛ Read out the following:

1   Height in class

2   Temperature change in a cup of tea over 20 minutes

3   Percentage of students for National Curriculum levels

4   Rainfall in a year

5   Amount of people with each type of games console

Answers

1 Bar chart   2 Line graph   3 Pie chart   4 Bar chart   5 Pie chart

Differentiation

⊛ ⇑ Use more ambiguous examples and ask the students to justify their choice. For example, traffic use on a road (bar versus pie).

Only average

Objective covered
F9f *In an investigation, derive new information from data, e.g. averages, probabilities.*

Aim
To be able to calculate averages using a spreadsheet package.

Resources
Computers with spreadsheet software.

Activity
⊛ Explain that one benefit of using a computer for calculations is that lots of calculations can be done very quickly.

⊛ Display the following data:

	A	B	C	D	E
1	22	24	26	25	35
2	45	43	42	44	44
3	33	35	32	31	37
4	11	14	13	11	12
5	56	52	57	54	55

⊛ Show the students that the formula to calculate an average is *=average(first cell:last cell)*.

⊛ Ask them to work out the formula to calculate the average for the top row: *=average(A1:E1)*. Check the formula by showing it working.

⊛ Demonstrate how to drag the formula down to calculate the averages for the other rows.

⊛ Ask them to do the same to calculate the column averages.

Differentiation
⊛ ⇓ Spend more time going through the formula on the board, explaining cell address and so on.

That's stats

Objective covered

F9g *In an investigation, check whether conclusions are plausible.*

Aim

To prove that data are not always plausible when averaged.

Activity

- Explain to the students that sometimes they should think carefully about what an average is proving.

- Go through the example of number of legs. Explain that while the majority of people have two legs, the national average is 1.998 because nobody has more than two, but some people do have less. Ask whether this means that some people have 1.998 legs.

- Ask the students to think of more examples like this. Other examples are number of wheels on a car or bike, wings on a plane, children in a family, televisions in a house.

- Ask them how they could phrase the results sensibly. For example, they should say that most families have two or three children, or they should round up or round down.

Differentiation

- ⇓ Stick to one example and emphasise why it makes no sense to say that the majority of people have 1.998 legs.

Apply the correct application

Objective covered

F6a *In an investigation, use software options and formats to store, retrieve and present electronic material efficiently.*

Aim

To know that data are often better stored in a spreadsheet than in a table or word processing package because they can be manipulated.

Resources

Computers with spreadsheet and word processing software.

Activity

⊛ Show a simple table produced using a spreadsheet and a word processor.

⊛ Show how they can be made to look the same using print preview.

⊛ Explain and show how you can sort, filter and produce a graph using the spreadsheet.

Differentiation

⊛ ⇑ Also compare to database software (include use of queries and forms).

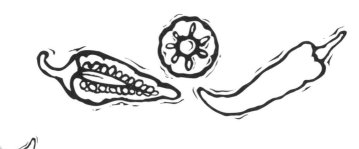

Cool down

Objective covered

F6b, F6c *In an investigation: explore and interpret collected data in order to draw conclusions; assess the consistency of conclusions with other evidence.*

Aim

To be able to interpret information from graphs and decide whether it agrees with what is already known.

Resources

OHP, board or worksheet prepared with graphs like these:

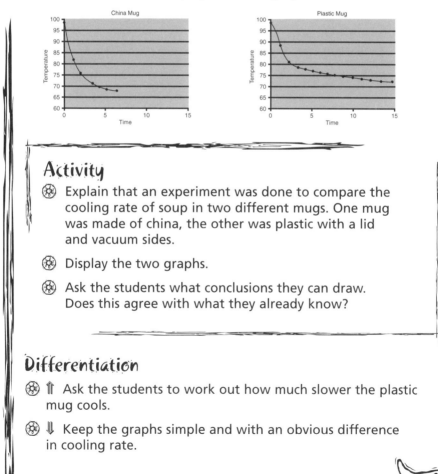

Activity

⊛ Explain that an experiment was done to compare the cooling rate of soup in two different mugs. One mug was made of china, the other was plastic with a lid and vacuum sides.

⊛ Display the two graphs.

⊛ Ask the students what conclusions they can draw. Does this agree with what they already know?

Differentiation

⊛ ⇑ Ask the students to work out how much slower the plastic mug cools.

⊛ ⇓ Keep the graphs simple and with an obvious difference in cooling rate.

EPOSible

Objective covered

F7a *Understand how data collection and storage are automated in commerce and some public services.*

Aim

To understand how an EPOS system works in a shop.

Resources

List of actions for display:

scan item
check data
set up system
write letter to supplier
update stock
data input
order new stock if low

Activity

⊛ Arrange the students into groups of three or four.

⊛ Ask the students to put the actions into the order in which they must happen.

Answers

1 set up system
2 data input
3 scan item
4 update stock
5 check data
6 order new stock if low
7 write letter to supplier

Differentiation

⊛ ⇑ Get the students to draw the answer as a flow chart using the correct symbols.

Is shopping easier?

Objective covered

F7b *Understand the impact of electronic databases on commercial practice and society.*

Aim

To know how EPOS and EFTPOS have changed shops and shopping.

Resources

Worksheets prepared with the following text.

EPOS and EFTPOS

EPOS stands for Electronic Point Of Sale. The system involves the use of barcodes and scanners at the till. Cashiers scan the barcode and the price is automatically transferred to the till. The number in stock is automatically reduced by one. The cashier has less chance of making a mistake and there is no need to count items on shelves. This system takes a long time to set up as every item needs to be input before it starts. Any mistake on input will be made every time the item is scanned until it is noticed.

EFTPOS stands for Electronic Fund Transfer at Point Of Sale. This involves the use of credit and debit cards. There is no need for customers to carry lots of cash as money is transferred from one account to another electronically. There are fewer mistakes as no one has to count money. If a card is stolen it can be stopped, so the money is not lost forever, but if it is not stopped, lots more money can be stolen. EFTPOS has allowed for many more points of sale, such as buying over the phone and Internet, but security is much more difficult here.

Activity

⊛ This is a DART activity.

⊛ Give the students a worksheet each. Ask them to underline all the advantages and circle all the disadvantages of EPOS and EFTPOS.

Differentiation

⊛ ⇑ More able students could summarise how this affects customers, employees and employers.

Specify the design

Objective covered
F3a *Construct, test and document the development of a database system which shows a design specification.*

Aim
To understand what a design specification is and to be able to use one to produce a database.

Resources
Display a design specification similar to the one below.

The database needs:
- film name (50 spaces)
- director's name (30 spaces)
- year of release (4 spaces)
- leading stars (50 spaces)
- number of copies (2 spaces)
- film rating (5 spaces)
- shop name (XpressVideo).

Activity
⊛ Explain that a design specification is a list of requirements for a package.

⊛ Tell the students that they have been asked to produce a database form for a video shop to store information about films.

⊛ Display the design specification.

⊛ Ask the students to design a data entry form using this design specification.

Differentiation
⊛ ⇓ Go through the process with the students step by step.

Verify or validate?

Objective covered

F3b *Construct, test and document the development of a database system which shows appropriate means of data input and validation.*

Aim

To understand the difference between validation and verification.

Resources

Cards with 'validation' written on one side and 'verification' on the other.

Activity

- ✸ Explain to the students that validation is a check on what is being entered into a computer as it is entered. For example, the computer will not accept 'purple' as a date as it is invalid.

- ✸ Explain that verification is checking information after it has been entered to make sure it makes sense. For example, age = 240 is valid, but it does not make sense.

- ✸ Hand out a card to each student.

- ✸ Read the following errors in a database to the students and ask them to use the cards to indicate whether they will be found by validation techniques or verification:

  1 Name is spelled incorrectly

  2 Date is written '19/969'

  3 Age is written 'twelve' not '12'

  4 Date of birth is '01/01/1734'

  5 Favourite car is written 'curry'

  6 House number is written 'Heron Farm'

Answers

1 Verification   2 Validation   3 Validation
4 Verification   5 Verification   6 Validation

Why it's no good

Objective covered

F3d *Construct, test and document the development of a database system which shows evaluation of the system's performance and suggested modifications.*

Aim

To know how to improve a database form and make it more effective.

Resources

Database form for display:

Name:	
Marital status:	
Department:	
Age:	
Hobbies:	

Activity

⊛ Explain that the form is used to make a database of employees working at a company. Employees are paid an amount related to how long they have been at the company. Those who work in the accounts department get paid more. The bosses want to know when staff birthdays are and what their hobbies are. They also want to know if they are married and have children.

⊛ Ask the students what information they cannot find and how the form could be improved.

Differentiation

⊛ ⇑ Ask the students to produce the database form on a computer (perhaps in a DTP package).

Follow the master

Objective covered

D1 *Use automated processes to increase efficiency (e.g. templates, master pages).*

Aim

To understand how using a 'house style' is beneficial to the user.

Resources

Company logos.
Computers with presentation software.

Activity

 Display some company logos. Ask the students what they are for. Explain that the symbol is part of the house style for a company.

 Discuss with the class what is important in creating a house style. Include colour, font and layout.

 Demonstrate how a house style can be incorporated into a presentation software package using a master slide.

Differentiation

 ⇑ Look at more than one example and compare.

Which way now?

Objective covered

D2 *Represent simple processes as diagrams, showing: how a task can be broken down into smaller ones; the sequence of operations, and any conditions or decisions that affect it; the initial information needed (e.g. room temperature, prices of items).*

Aim

To understand how to sequence instructions to direct a person around a classroom.

Resources

Blindfold.

Activity

- Explain to the class that all computer programs are made of sequenced commands.

- Ask for a volunteer, and blindfold them.

- Command the volunteer around the class using verbal instructions. At first issue one command at a time, then build up to several commands at a time (a program).

Differentiation

- ⇑ Ask one student to direct. Include more detailed instructions such as 'sit down' and 'pick up'.

- ⇓ Only use simple instructions such as 'forward', 'back', 'left' and 'right'.

Clever signals

Objective covered
D2b *Represent simple processes as diagrams, showing the sequence of operations, and any conditions or decisions that affect it.*

Aim
To understand the factors that affect the way traffic lights are timed.

Activity
- ✹ Draw a bird's eye view of a narrow bridge on the board. Ask the students how best to organise traffic to go over it. (Try to prompt 'use of traffic lights'.)

- ✹ Explain that the bridge is on the way into a large town. Ask the students how this affects the traffic. (Traffic flows heavily in one direction in the morning and the other in the evening.)

- ✹ Discuss how to solve the problem of traffic build up during these hours. Get the students to think about using timings and/or sensors.

Differentiation
- ✹ ⇑ The students could think about a crossroads with pedestrian crossings.

- ✹ ⇓ Use a level crossing as it is very clear that either cars move or trains move.

Ticket time

Objective covered

D1a *Automate simple processes by creating templates.*

Aim

To be able to design a ticket for a school production.

Activity

⊛ Tell the students that they are going to design a ticket for a school play.

⊛ Brainstorm on the board with the class all the information that is needed on the ticket. Some examples are name of production, date, price, seat number and venue.

⊛ Ask the students to design the ticket (on paper) so that the template is easy to adapt for future productions.

Differentiation

⊛ ⇑ The students could try to design the ticket on a computer.

⊛ ⇓ Write the information needed on the board and ask the students to design the ticket.

⊛ ⇓ Give the students a 'blank ticket' worksheet to fill in.

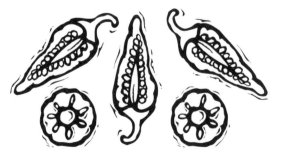

You've got style

Objective covered

D1a, D1b *Automate simple processes by creating templates and creating simple software routines (e.g. style sheets, web queries, control techniques on web pages).*

Aim

To be able to design a general league table for inter-tutor group sports.

Resources

Computers with spreadsheet software.

Activity

⚽ Ask the students to use a spreadsheet to design a template for any inter-tutor group sports competition like the one below.

Inter-Tutor Group League Table: Football					
Tutor Group	Played	Won	Drawn	Lost	Points
B1	4	4	0	0	12
B2	4	3	0	1	9
B3	4	1	1	2	4
B4	4	0	0	4	0
B5	4	2	1	1	7

⚽ Explain that this is called a style sheet and it is a template that can be used for more than one purpose (many different sports and activities).

Differentiation

⚽ ⇑ Ask the students to include the formulae needed and explain how to sort the information.

⚽ ⇓ Give the headings for the columns on the board.

Out of order

Objective covered
D2 *Consider the benefits and drawbacks of using ICT to automate processes (e.g. using wizards, templates).*

Aim
To understand that ICT is not always the most appropriate method of completing a task.

Resources
Computers with software that includes poster templates (e.g. DTP).

Activity
⊛ Tell the students that they are going to produce an 'out of order' poster on a computer.

⊛ Split the class in half. Ask one half to make the poster using a template, the other half to start from a blank page. While they are doing this, you should produce a similar poster with pen and paper.

⊛ Discuss which of the three ways is the most appropriate for the purpose – the pen and paper was quicker and did the job, albeit with a less professional finish.

Differentiation
⊛ ⇓ Make it a race and split the class into three groups

That's a state!

Objective covered

D3 *Represent simple design specifications as diagrams.*

Aim

To understand that a routine task often needs a template.

Resources

Plain A4 paper.

Activity

⊛ Ask the students to brainstorm what they would need to include on a poster to advertise a house. List their ideas on the board.

⊛ Ask them to hand draw an A4 advert for a house showing where they would put the title, picture, price, phone number, address, company logo and other information about the house.

Differentiation

⊛ ⇑ Ask the students to complete the task without brainstorming. Discuss and compare posters when they have finished.

⊛ ⇓ Complete the task as a class on the board asking 'Where should I put...?'

Merge it

Objective covered

D1 *Automate ICT processes (e.g. use software to merge mail, create macros in an application program).*

Aim

To understand what a mail merge is and how it works.

Resources

Post-it notes.
Board prepared with this letter and 'print button'.

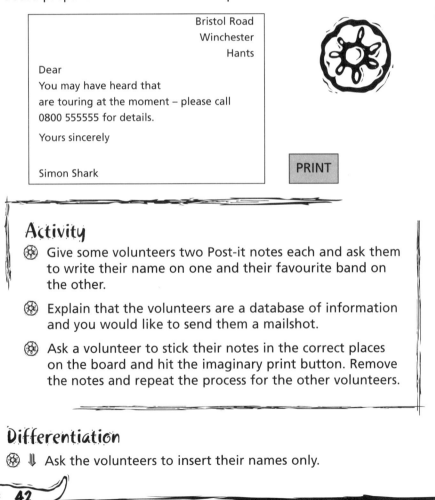

```
                              Bristol Road
                               Winchester
                                    Hants
      Dear
      You may have heard that
      are touring at the moment – please call
      0800 555555 for details.

      Yours sincerely


      Simon Shark
```

PRINT

Activity

- ✸ Give some volunteers two Post-it notes each and ask them to write their name on one and their favourite band on the other.

- ✸ Explain that the volunteers are a database of information and you would like to send them a mailshot.

- ✸ Ask a volunteer to stick their notes in the correct places on the board and hit the imaginary print button. Remove the notes and repeat the process for the other volunteers.

Differentiation

- ✸ ⇓ Ask the volunteers to insert their names only.

Home sweet home

Objective covered
D1 *Automate ICT processes (e.g. use software to merge mail, create macros in an application program).*

Aim
To understand what a macro is.

Resources
Different coloured washable spirit pens

Activity
- ❋ Write the numbers 1 to 7 evenly spaced on the board.
- ❋ Ask for three volunteers. Give each a different coloured pen and tell them the following instructions (or give them instruction cards):

  1 Draw a square above the number 1.

  2 Draw a triangle directly on top of the square.

  3 Draw two windows and a door in the square.

- ❋ Ask other volunteers to repeat the task at the other numbers on the board.
- ❋ Explain that the volunteers have been a macro and that a routine task can be repeated with very simple instructions.

Differentiation
- ❋ ⇓ Use less complicated instructions to complete a simpler task, such as a number in a circle in a square.

Keep it simple, stupid

Objective covered

D2 *Represent a system in a diagram, identifying all its parts, including inputs, outputs and the processes used (e.g. to validate data).*

Aim

To understand the importance of using non-technical language at times.

Activity

✳ Ask the students to write down how the school library system works without using any technical terms such as scan, database, records, input, output or update.

Differentiation

✳ ⇩ Draw or display a flow chart to help the students before they start.

✳ ⇩ Give the students a writing frame to use.

Easy as boiling an egg

Objective covered

D2 *Represent a system in a diagram, identifying all its parts, including inputs, outputs and the processes used (e.g. to validate data).*

Aim

To be able to put instructions in order.

Resources

Flow chart cards prepared with the instructions to boil an egg (see below).
Blu-Tack.

Activity

* Show the students some of the cards to introduce them to the correct flow chart symbols.

* Stick the cards to the board. Get the students to tell you the order that they should go in.

Answers

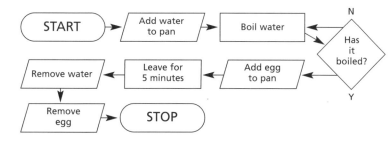

Differentiation

* ⬆ Use detailed instructions and ask students to spot 'bugs' in the system. For example, what if the pan is already full of water?

* ⬇ Ignore the flow chart shapes and design the cards so that they only fit together in the correct order.

I've got your number

Objective covered

D3a *Use software to investigate and amend a simple model by formatting and labelling data appropriately (e.g. formatting cells to display currency).*

Aim

To know that it is important to enter information correctly so that it can be manipulated at a later date.

Activity

⊛ Brainstorm with the class the information that a shop needs to keep about its staff in order to pay them. Ideas could include name, date started, amount paid, bank number, hours worked and staff ID number.

⊛ Ask the students what type of information each would be and how they would format the cells/fields. Explain the benefits of this for sorting and validation. (Sorting – numbers written as words can be sorted alphabetically. Calculations – cannot add up numbers written as words. Validation – allows correct input only.)

Answers

Name (text), date started (date/time), amount paid (currency), bank number (number), hours worked (number), staff ID number (autonumber/number)

Differentiation

⊛ ⇓ Only use one example of each type of information. List these for the students.

Plan it properly

Objective covered

D3a *Use software to investigate and amend a simple model by formatting and labelling data appropriately (e.g. formatting cells to display currency).*

Aim

To know how to set up a database to expect the correct type of information.

Resources

Sets of cards prepared with the following:

Text	Number	Date/time

Activity

⊛ Ask the students to brainstorm the information they would put in a diary to organise their day, for example event, time, date, location and who with. List their ideas on the board.

⊛ Give each student a set of cards. Ask them to hold up which one they think would be appropriate for each piece of information on the board as you read it out. Explain that this is important for sorting information and doing calculations.

⊛ Also, ask the students how big the field should be to guarantee it will contain all the information.

Differentiation

⊛ ⇑ Try more complex information and add more cards, for example 'autonumber'.

⊛ ⇓ Use the same cards, but ask the students what information is needed in an address book.

What comes next?

Objective covered

D3b Use software to investigate and amend a simple model by entering rules or formulae and checking their appropriateness and accurate working.

Aim

To be able to spot a pattern in groups of numbers and use a simple formula.

Resources

Computers with spreadsheet software.

Activity

⊛ Display the following spreadsheet and ask the students to copy it.

	A	B	C
1	10	10	100
2	20	20	400
3	30	30	900
4	40	40	?

⊛ Ask the students to predict what should be in cell C4 by looking at the pattern in the numbers.

⊛ Ask the students to enter a formula into the cell to check their answer.

Answers

1600 (=A4*B4)

Differentiation

⊛ ⇑ Add extra rows, for example 50*50 and 60*60.

⊛ ⇑ Leave more gaps so that only one complete row is showing.

⊛ ⇑ Choose a more complex pattern.

⊛ ⇓ Use easier numbers and use addition instead of multiplication.

Profit or loss?

Objective covered

D3c *Use software to investigate and amend a simple model by explaining the rules governing a model.*

Aim

To understand how a profit/loss spreadsheet can be constructed.

Resources

Computers with spreadsheet software.

Activity

⊛ Explain to the class the meaning of 'profit' and 'loss'.

⊛ Display the following spreadsheet:

	A	B	C	D
1		Income	Outgoing	
2	Coach		300	
3	Ticket		400	
4	Hotel		600	
5	Food		200	
6	Adult tickets	700		
7	Child tickets	900		
8	Family tickets	500		
9	Totals	2100	1500	
10	Profit			600

⊛ Ask the students to work out where a formula should be used and what it might be.

Answers

B9=SUM(B2:B8), C9=SUM(C2:C8), D10=B9-C9

Differentiation

⊛ ⇓ Treat this as a teacher-led task and talk the class through each step on the board.

Party time

Objective covered

D3d *Use software to investigate and amend a simple model by predicting the effects of changing variables or rules.*

Aim

To predict the effect of changing variables and rules.

Activity

⊛ Tell the students that they have won the Lottery and that they are going to celebrate by having a party for their friends. They have £200 to spend on food and drink.

⊛ Open the pre-prepared spreadsheet 'Party', as below.

Item	Number bought	Price each	Amount spent on this item
Slices of pizza		£0.45	£0.00
Sausages on a stick		£0.06	£0.00
Cheese & pineapple		£0.03	£0.00
Chicken wings		£0.61	£0.00
Cream gateaux		£4.99	£0.00
Cake		£3.99	£0.00
Coke		£1.99	£0.00
Sprite		£1.52	£0.00
Fanta		£1.99	£0.00
Orange juice		£2.99	£0.00
	Total money spent		£0.00
	Amount of money left		£200.00

⊛ Working in pairs, students need to vary the number bought in order to get as close to £200 as possible. Prompt them to discuss how they are deciding what to change.

Differentiation

⊛ ⇑ Prepare a spreadsheet with more variables, such as different brands of cake with different prices.

⊛ ⇑ Ask students to explain why ICT is more effective than other methods.

⊛ ⇓ As a class, evelute items to decide whether the food chosen is suitable for a party.

A better deal

Objective covered
D3d *Use software to investigate and amend a simple model by predicting the effects of changing variables or rules.*

Aim
To understand the principles of changing the variables and the effect this can have.

Resources
Computers with spreadsheet software.

Activity
 Display the spreadsheet from 'Profit or loss?', page 49. Tell the students that a cheaper hotel has been found.

 Ask the students how changing the 'cost of hotel' variable to £400 will affect the other cells in the spreadsheet. Ask them which cells will change and what they will become.

Answers
Cell C9 will become 1300 and cell D10 will become 800.

Differentiation
Change more than one variable.

Dodgy dealers

Objective covered

D4 *Test whether a simple model operates satisfactorily.*

Aim

To be able to check that a formula has been set up correctly in a spreadsheet.

Resources

The following table, which shows the prices of two cars:

	Cost	Quantity 1	Total 1	Quantity 2	Total 2
Price of car	10 000	1	10 000	1	10 000
Power steering	300	1	300	1	300
Sunroof	500	0	0	1	500
Electric windows	150	1	150	0	0
Air conditioning	800	0	0	1	800
CD player	200	1	200	1	200
			10 650		11 000

Activity

✸ Ask the students to check which car is totalled correctly and which has a mistake in the formula.

Differentiation

✸ ⇑ Give no help with the calculation.

✸ ⇓ Explain estimation and go through the calculations with the class (or allow them to use calculators).

Cheapskate

Objective covered
D5 *Draw and explain conclusions (e.g. 'the best value for money is obtained when...').*

Aim
To be able to decide which offer is better value when given a number of options.

Resources
Table prepared for display:

Item	Cost
Plate	£3.00
Side plate	£1.00
Cup	£2.00
Saucer	£1.50
Bowl	£2.50
1 complete set	£8.00
6 complete sets	£50.00

Activity
- ✳ Ask the students how they would choose to buy enough crockery for eight people. Ask them how much it would cost.

- ✳ Then set these three questions:

  1. How much would eight sets cost if the items were bought individually?
  2. How much would eight sets cost if they were bought as eight complete sets?
  3. Which is the cheapest method of purchase?

Answers
1 £80   2 £64   3 Eight complete sets

Differentiation
- ✳ ⇑ Ask the students to add columns such as 'quantity' and 'sub total' to work out costs on a spreadsheet.

- ✳ ⇓ Leave out the '6 complete sets' option.

Top of the class

Objective covered
D6 *Review and modify ICT models to improve their accuracy and extend their scope (e.g. by introducing different or new variables and producing further outcomes).*

Aim
To be able to sort (and rank) data on a spreadsheet.

Resources
Computers with spreadsheet software.
The spreadsheet below displayed on the board or on individual workstations from a shared area.

	A	B	C	D
1		English	Maths	Science
2	Rachel	18	19	4
3	Max	20	5	15
4	Dave	20	10	18
5	Nesrene	15	16	7
6	Andy	16	15	18

Activity
⊛ Ask the students a few questions, such as 'Who is top in maths?'

⊛ Ask when this might be hard to find out (lots of data) and demonstrate sorting one subject by column using the Data/Sort function.

⊛ Ask the students to sort the columns for the other two subjects.

Differentiation
⊛ ⇑ Ask the students to rank the information. The formula for E2 to sort by science would be =RANK(D2,$D$2:$D$6,0).

⊛ ⇓ Demonstrate only, explaining each step as you go.

Bug in my tea

Objective covered
D3 *Design and create ICT-based models, testing and refining rules or procedures.*

Aim
To understand that flow diagrams always need checking and to know what kind of errors to look for.

Resources
OHP or board prepared with the following flow chart:

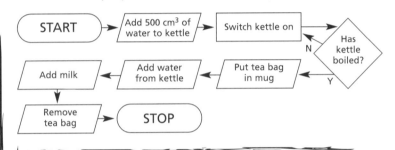

Activity
- Ask the students to spot any potential bugs in the system shown by the flow chart. They might need one example to get them started.
- Ask them to correct the flow chart to remove the bugs.

Answers
Check kettle is empty first.
Is mug empty/clean?
How much water/milk in mug?
Is the tea the correct strength?
Sugar?

Differentiation
- ⇓ Talk the students through the flow chart. At each step try to prompt them about bugs.

Science is cool

Objective covered

D4 *Test hypotheses and predictions using models, comparing their behaviour with information from other sources.*

Aim

To be able to test whether a statement is true by looking at the results of an experiment.

Resources

Table prepared for display:

Volume = 200 cm³		Volume = 400 cm³	
Temp (°C)	Time (s)	Temp (°C)	Time (s)
100	0	100	0
90	15	90	38
80	35	80	88
70	65	70	163
60	115	60	288
50	185	50	463

Activity

⊛ Explain that in science, a student has made the hypothesis that if you double the volume of boiling water, it will take twice as long to cool.

⊛ Ask the class whether they think the student is right by showing them the data in the table.

⊛ Ask the students how they worked out the answer.

Answers

No, double 185 is 370 not 463.

Differentiation

⊛ ⇑ Ask the students to work out what the relationship is. (It takes 2.5 times longer.)

⊛ ⇓ Make it more obvious by recording the temperature at certain times so that the table is bigger for 400 cm³.

Speed trap

Objective covered
D5 *Implement a system to carry out a simple control task, including some that involve sensed physical data.*

Aim
To know how to measure the speed of a moving vehicle.

Activity
- ✹ Ask the students what speed is measured in (mph, km/h).

- ✹ Explain that this means that two important factors are distance and time.

- ✹ Ask the students what equipment they would need to measure speed (stopwatch, metre rule and so on). Prompt them to think of ICT-based equipment such as pressure sensors, light sensors and electronic timers.

- ✹ Explain with the use of a diagram how to set up a system to measure the speed of a moving vehicle:

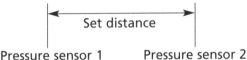

Set distance

Pressure sensor 1   Pressure sensor 2

- ✹ Tell the students that they would need to measure the time taken for the vehicle to travel between the two pressure sensors, which are a set distance apart.

- ✹ Explain that the speed of the vehicle can then be worked out using the formula 'speed = distance ÷ time'.

Differentiation
- ✹ ⇑ After the activity, discuss when it is appropriate to use a stopwatch and metre rule (for slow speeds like walking).

- ✹ ⇓ Start with the diagram and explain the system.

In a spin

Objective covered

D5a *Implement a system to carry out a simple control task, including some that involve sensed physical data, by compiling sets of instructions, identifying those which can be grouped to form procedures or loops.*

Aim

To understand how systems flow and where there are loops in a system.

Activity

⚙ Brainstorm with the class all the tasks done by a washing machine in a cycle. Ideas should include add water, heat water, add powder, add conditioner, rinse, soak, fast spin and tumble.

⚙ Ask the class to get into pairs. They should try to create a flow chart showing the sequence of the washing machine cycle.

Answers

The correct order for the tasks is: add water, add powder, heat water, soak, tumble, add conditioner, rinse, fast spin.

Differentiation

⚙ ⇑ Give the students minimum help (phrases only).

⚙ ⇑ Ask them to identify loops in the system, for example reaching correct temperature.

⚙ ⇓ Put the instructions on the board or on shaped cards that only fit together in the correct order.

⚙ ⇓ Ask eight volunteers to act out the different roles and get into the correct order.

Library loop

Objective covered

D5a *Implement a system to carry out a simple control task, including some that involve sensed physical data, by compiling sets of instructions, identifying those which can be grouped to form procedures or loops.*

Aim

To understand how systems flow and where there are loops in a system.

Resources

OHP or board prepared with the basic journey (shown as solid lines) of a book taken from a library:

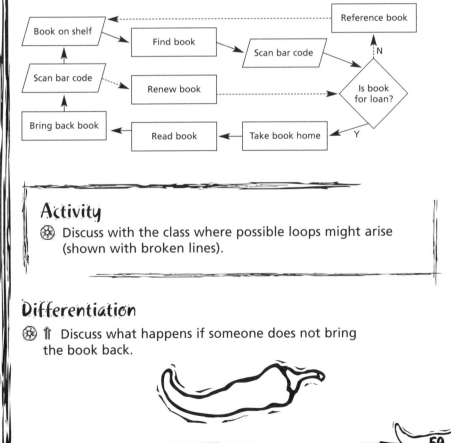

Activity

✿ Discuss with the class where possible loops might arise (shown with broken lines).

Differentiation

✿ ⇑ Discuss what happens if someone does not bring the book back.

Making a procedure

Objective covered

D5a *Implement a system to carry out a simple control task, including some that involve sensed physical data, by compiling sets of instructions, identifying those which can be grouped to form procedures or loops.*

Aim

To understand how to make a set of instructions to perform a task.

Activity

- Explain to the students what a command is, for example 'stand up'.

- Ask the students to produce a list of commands to explain how to go somewhere (such as the room next door) from their seat. For example: stand up, turn left, walk forward five paces, turn left, open door and so on.

Differentiation

- ⇓ Choose a simple task such as 'stand up', 'walk to desk', 'pick up something'.

Why can't I shop?

Objective covered

D5b *Implement a system to carry out a simple control task, including some that involve sensed physical data, by testing and refining the instructions.*

Aim

To be able to spot errors and problems in a sequence of instructions.

Activity

⊛ Show the students the following procedure to go shopping to buy a birthday present. Tell them that it has been tested and was found not to work.

1 Get into car
2 Drive to shop
3 Park
4 Put money in machine
5 Get ticket
6 Go to shop
7 Find present
8 Go to car
9 Drive home

⊛ Ask the students to work in groups. They should write down all the errors they can find and the problems that will occur as a result.

⊛ As a class, discuss the errors and add commands to the procedure to solve the problems.

Answers

There are many commands missing: unlock car, drive to car park, how much money? display ticket in window, lock car, go to checkout, buy present, unlock car, get into car.

Differentiation

⊛ ⇑ The students should add the commands in their groups.

⊛ ⇓ Perform the whole task as a class.

Fast and furious

Objective covered
D7a *Develop and test a system to monitor and control events by using sensors efficiently.*

Aim
To be able to select the correct type of sensor for a specific task.

Activity
⊛ Write the following on the board:

light sensor   pressure sensor   heat sensor   sound sensor

⊛ Ask the students to think about how each sensor works. Discuss the type of vehicles and the speed of traffic that can be measured by each sensor.

Answers
Light sensor – a beam is cut for longer for a larger vehicle (but also a slower vehicle).
Pressure sensor – larger pressure for larger vehicle, shorter peak for faster vehicle.
Heat sensor – larger engine, more heat given off.
Sound sensor – larger noise, larger vehicle.

Differentiation
⊛ ⇑ Ask the students to predict what a graph of the results would look like for different vehicles.

⊛ ⇓ Tell the class how each sensor works and then get them to decide which they would use for different vehicles.

You doughnut!

Objective covered

D7b *Develop and test a system to monitor and control events by developing, testing and refining efficient sequences of instructions and procedures.*

Aim

To understand that repeating procedures is often the most efficient method of completing a task.

Activity

⊛ Write on the board the process for making a doughnut:

1   Make dough

2   Roll into ball

3   Cook

4   Add jam

5   Add sugar

⊛ Explain that if you are making one doughnut, one person can do all these tasks. Ask what problems you might get if you make 10 doughnuts by this method (people get in each other's way).

⊛ Try to prompt the students to come up with the solution that it is better if one person does the same task over and over.

⊛ Explain that computers also often repeat tasks to make them more efficient.

Differentiation

⊛ ⇑ Discuss where bottlenecks occur in the system (making dough and cooking) and ask why it is important to know this (to avoid a pile up).

⊛ ⇓ Use cards and act out the process in role-play.

Once is an oeuf

Objective covered

D7b *Develop and test a system to monitor and control events by developing, testing and refining efficient sequences of instructions and procedures.*

Aim

To be able to use procedures to draw an outline of the French flag.

Activity

❀ Draw an outline of the French flag on the board. Alongside the outline, write the procedures to draw it:

fd 100, rt 90, fd 180, rt 90,
fd 100, rt 90, fd 60, rt 90,
fd 100, bk 100, lt 90, fd 60,
rt 90, fd 100, bk 100, lt 90,
fd 60

❀ Ask the students how repeating commands could make it easier. Try to prompt them that this can be done by repeating lines to make a rectangle.

=repeat 2[fd 100 rt 90 fd 60 rt 90]

Differentiation

❀ ⇑ Discuss how a procedure called 'rectangle' could be repeated to draw a flag:

rectangle =repeat 2[fd 100 rt 90 fd 60 rt 90]

Repeat this three times moving the cursor between repeats.

No trainers, no jeans

Objective covered
D5a *Use ICT to build and test an efficient system to monitor and control events, including testing all elements of the system using appropriate test data.*

Aim
To understand how AND and OR gates function in a system.

Activity
- Explain to the students that they are bouncers for a nightclub with strict dress codes. The rules are:

  Monday – no dress code

  Tuesday – no dress code

  Wednesday – no dress code

  Thursday – no trainers, no jeans

  Friday – no trainers, no jeans

  Saturday – no trainers, no jeans, ties required for men

  Sunday – closed

- Write these rules on the board and set up a few scenarios to see if the bouncer should allow entry, for example:

  1   A student wearing jeans tries to enter on a Thursday.

  2   A woman in trainers tries to enter on a Monday.

- Ask the students to write the rules using AND and OR gates.

Answers
(jeans OR trainers) AND (Thursday OR Friday OR Saturday) = no entry

Differentiation
- ⇓ Try the task in reverse; give the students the rules as AND and OR gates and ask them to interpret the rules for each day.

Bottlenecks and breakdowns

Objective covered

D5b *Use ICT to build and test an efficient system to monitor and control events, including evaluating the system's performance.*

Aim

To know what makes a good system and what problems can arise.

Activity

⊛ Ask the students to think of a system used in everyday life. A good example would be a car park. Ask them what a good system in a car park is.

⊛ Ask what would make a bad system, what problems there are and how these can be avoided. Try to prompt the students to think of bottlenecks in the system. Describe the two systems shown below:

1 Collect ticket, enter car park, park, return to car park, enter ticket, pay required amount, collect ticket, return to car, drive to exit, enter ticket, leave

2 Collect ticket, enter car park, park, return to car park, drive to exit, enter ticket, pay required amount, leave

⊛ Tell the students that there are fewer steps in the second system. Do they think it is as good? Try to prompt them to think of the choice of one long queue versus two shorter queues. Which is less frustrating?

Differentiation

⊛ ⇑ Ask the students to come up with two different versions of another system.

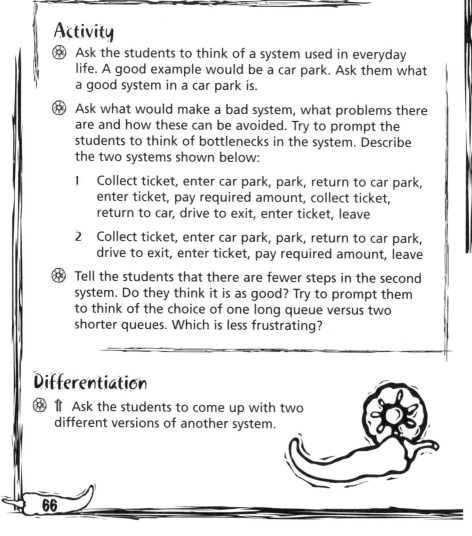

User-friendly user guides

Objective covered

D5c *Use ICT to build and test an efficient system to monitor and control events, including annotating work to highlight processes and justify decisions.*

Aim

To know what is important to include in a user guide.

Activity

- ✺ Explain to the students what a user guide is. Ask them to decide the purpose of a user guide and what the target audience should be.

- ✺ Arrange the students into groups of three or four.

- ✺ Ask them to brainstorm the important factors in writing a user guide. Give an example to start them off, for example, the language should not be too technical.

- ✺ Ask them to decide what factors are most important and make a list from most to least important.

Answers

Diagrams needed to help explanation. All common problems described with solutions in troubleshooting section. Needs to explain how to set up system. Needs to explain how to use the system. Should be in correct language for target audience. Needs to be broken down into tasks. Should have a good contents page and index.

Differentiation

- ✺ ⇓ Give the students the important factors and ask them to rank them in order.

Need a better form?

Objective covered

D6 *Review and modify own or other's monitoring and control systems to improve efficiency (e.g. use more efficient procedures, reduce the number of instructions or procedures, add an element of feedback).*

Aim

To be able to improve a data input form on a database.

Resources

Data input form:

Customer name:	Paper deliveries database
ID number:	Paper boy
Newspaper:	
Name of paper:	Last paid?

Activity

- ⊛ Display the form and ask the students to point out all the bad points.

- ⊛ Then ask the students to design, on paper, their own improved form to input the same information.

Differentiation

⊛ ⇑ More able students could produce the design on a database package.

Too tricky

Objective covered

D6 *Review and modify own or other's monitoring and control systems to improve efficiency (e.g. use more efficient procedures, reduce the number of instructions or procedures, add an element of feedback).*

Aim

To be able to reduce the number of algorithms in a flow chart to make it simpler.

Resources

Flow chart for display:

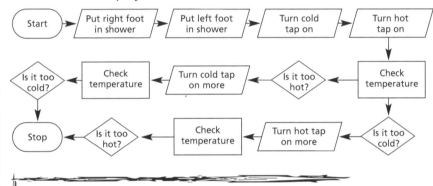

Activity

⊛ Ask the students to design a flow chart to monitor shower temperature without using so many commands. Can they simplify it? Can they make it work properly?

Answers

The tasks at the start could be improved with, for example, 'get into shower' and 'turn taps on'. Feedback loops need to be introduced after checking temperature.

Differentiation

⊛ ⇓ Lead the students through the tasks as you write the improved flow chart on the board.

Application of numbers

Objective covered
E1 *Recognise common forms and conventions used in communications and how these address audience needs (e.g. columns of text in newspapers, graphics and enlarged print in posters, hyperlinks on websites).*

Aim
To be able to recognise the purpose of a number from its format.

Activity
 Display the following list of numbers:

07970 555555	3b	29/06/1972	03:00
BS4 2QD	6'1"	2002/3	£4.50

 The students should get into pairs. Ask them to decide what the numbers are for by looking at their style.

Answers

Telephone number	Flat number	Date	Time
Postcode	Height	Academic year	Price

Differentiation
 ⇓ Give the students an example first. Write the answers randomly on the board to give them a choice.

What goes where?

Objective covered

E2 *Apply understanding of common forms and conventions to own ICT work.*

Aim

To be able to use text and numbers in the correct format to make them immediately recognisable.

Resources

Prepared worksheets similar to the one below.

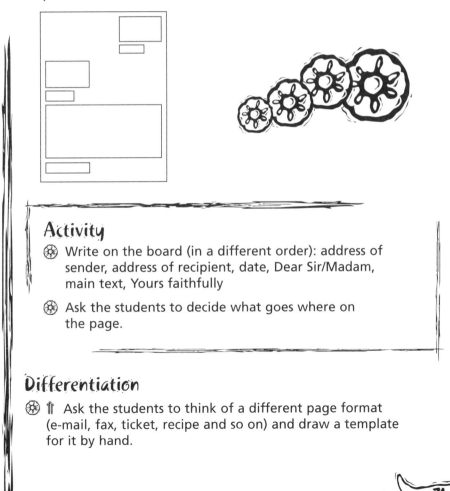

Activity

⊛ Write on the board (in a different order): address of sender, address of recipient, date, Dear Sir/Madam, main text, Yours faithfully

⊛ Ask the students to decide what goes where on the page.

Differentiation

⊛ ⇑ Ask the students to think of a different page format (e-mail, fax, ticket, recipe and so on) and draw a template for it by hand.

Effective flyers

Objective covered
E3 *Use given criteria to evaluate the effectiveness of own and others' publications and presentations.*

Aim
To be able to evaluate the effectiveness of different styles of presentation.

Resources
Two different flyers (A and B) for a similar event or product, preferably enlarged in colour.

Activity
⊛ Show the students the flyers.

⊛ The students should get into pairs. Ask them to list five good things and five bad about each flyer.

⊛ Tell the students that they need to choose a company to produce a flyer for a party. Ask them whether they would choose the company that made flyer A or B.

Differentiation
⊛ ⇑ Using their lists of good points, ask the students to design a flyer for a school disco by hand.

⊛ ⇓ Choose three points and do the task as a class discussion.

Who's it for?

Objective covered

E1 *Recognise how different media and presentation techniques convey similar content in ways that have different impacts.*

Aim

To understand how the same material can be adapted for different audiences using different presentation techniques.

Resources

A video of *Newsround* and a main evening news programme from the same day.

Activity

- ⊛ Show the students both videos and ask them to list five differences between the programmes individually.

- ⊛ Collect the differences from a selection of students, listing them on the board.

- ⊛ As a whole class, discuss why these differences are there and the effect this has on the target audience.

Differentiation

- ⊛ ⇑ Compare to a newspaper from the following morning with the same stories. Ask the students to think how the impact on the audience differs.

- ⊛ ⇓ Concentrate on one news item only.

Getting the point across

Objective covered

E1 *Recognise how different media and presentation techniques convey similar content in ways that have different impacts.*

Aim

To understand the benefits of presentation software by comparing it with an overhead transparency.

Resources

Computers with presentation software.
Use presentation software to prepare a three-slide presentation on a subject familiar to the students. Incorporate animations, sounds and transitions.
OHP and presentation slides printed on OHTs.

Activity

⊛ Show the students the presentation using both methods and discuss the benefits of using presentation software. Prompt them to think about attention span, ease of transition and so on.

Differentiation

⊛ ⇑ Discuss the benefits of OHT, such as portability, cost, ease of use and technical ability required of the presenter.

Weather it is right

Objective covered

E2 *Understand that an effective presentation or publication will address audience expectations and needs (e.g. the audience's levels of literacy, familiarity with a topic).*

Aims

To evaluate two different presentations of the same information for different audiences.

Activity

- ✹ Display a copy of *The Times* weather forecast for the day (either photocopies or a scanned image projected onto a screen).

- ✹ Brainstorm with the class the good and bad points of the presentation. Ask them to decide who they think the forecast is designed for and why.

- ✹ Display a copy of *The Sun* weather forecast for the day. Again discuss the good and bad points of the presentation. The students should be encouraged to talk about the differences between the presentations and how this target audience differs from the previous audience.

- ✹ Ask students: 'Why are they different? Which is better?'

Differentiation

- ✹ ⇑ Include cuttings from more papers, for example local papers.

- ✹ ⇑ Ask the students to decide whether news broadcasts are targeted at different audiences (discuss in small groups).

Choosing colours

Objective covered

E1a *Produce high quality ICT-based presentations by creating clear presentations, sensitive to audience needs.*

Aim

To understand that the use of colour has an effect on people's preconceived ideas.

Activity

⊛ On the board, brainstorm shops that have red, blue or yellow in their logos. Prompt ideas such as Spar, Tesco, IKEA, McDonald's, Boots, Woolworths and Pizza Hut.

⊛ Explain that these colours all represent cheap and cheerful images.

⊛ Brainstorm shops with green, gold and navy blue in their logos, such as Harrods, House of Fraser, The Body Shop, Laura Ashley, Timberland, John Lewis, Marks and Spencer and Burberry.

⊛ Explain that these colours suggest quality and luxury.

⊛ Ask the students to decide what colour they would suggest a local fast food restaurant used for their corporate image.

Differentiation

⊛ ⇑ Ask the students to design an 'opening soon' poster for a posh restaurant and another for a fast food restaurant. They should do this by hand, detailing the colours used.

Stranger danger

Objective covered
E1a *Produce high quality ICT-based presentations by creating clear presentations, sensitive to audience needs.*

Aim
To understand the importance of taking the audience into account when designing a leaflet.

Activity
- Explain that you are going to design a leaflet to warn 4-year-old children about the dangers of strangers.

- Brainstorm with the students five things that you must take into account. Ideas may include size of text, type of language, size of image, not too scary, type of image, memorable catch phrase and very clear point made.

- Draw on the board the outline of the leaflet. Ask the students what to put where.

Differentiation
Get the students to design the leaflet in small groups.

Well presented

Objective covered

E2 *Use knowledge of publications and media forms to devise criteria to assess the quality and impact of multimedia communications and presentations, and apply the criteria to develop and refine own work.*

Aim

To understand what makes a good presentation.

Activity

⊛ On the board, draw the centre of a spider diagram entitled 'A good presentation'.

⊛ Ask the students to add important points to consider when trying to produce a good presentation. Ideas may include colour, layout, animation, amount of text, size of text, use of image, transition and sound.

Differentiation

⊛ ⇑ Get the students to produce spider diagrams in pairs.

⊛ ⇓ Give two or three examples on the initial spider diagram to get the class started.

Judge a book by its cover

Objective covered

E4 *Plan and design the presentation of information in digital media, taking account of the purpose of the presentation and intended audience.*

Aim

To be able to judge the content of a book by looking at the style of the cover.

Resources

Five book covers, each from a different genre, for example horror, murder mystery, sci-fi, romance, war, comedy or children's.

Activity

- ✦ Display the five book covers.

- ✦ Arrange the students into small groups. Ask them to decide what genre each book belongs to. They should give five reasons for each decision.

Differentiation

- ✦ ⇑ Choose books that are less obviously one genre or another.

- ✦ ⇓ List the genres on the board for the students to choose from.

A good film?

Objective covered

E4 *Plan and design the presentation of information in digital media, taking account of the purpose of the presentation and intended audience.*

Aim

To be able to guess from a poster what a film is like and the audience it is designed for.

Resources

A film poster from a lesser-known film (could be downloaded from websites such as www.movieposters.com or www.amazon.co.uk).

Activity

⊛ Display the film poster.

⊛ Ask the students what they think the genre of the film is and why.

⊛ Ask them what they think the target audience is and why.

Differentiation

⊛ ⇑ Get the students to work in small groups, each looking at a different poster.

⊛ ⇓ Give the students some options to choose from, such as horror film for teens or horror film for adults.

⊛ ⇓ Choose a better-known film.

Right writing

Objective covered

E4 *Plan and design the presentation of information in digital media, taking account of the purpose of the presentation and intended audience.*

Aim

To understand why you might choose a certain font for a presentation.

Resources

The word 'Welcome' written in these types of fonts:

Welcome	creepy	Escalido Streak
Welcome	happy	Postino
Welcome	techno	OCRA Alternate
WELCOME	stencil	Stencil
Welcome	normal	Comic Sans

Activity

✸ The students should get into pairs. Ask them to decide when they would use each font, what it would sound like if they said it, and what atmosphere it evokes.

Differentiation

✸ ⇑ Ask the students to choose a word and write it in five different styles to evoke five different feelings.

✸ ⇓ Say the word to the students in such a way that you prompt the correct response.

Colouring clipart

Objective covered

E5b *Use ICT to draft and refine a presentation, including reorganising, developing and combining information, including text, images and sound, using the simple editing functions of common applications.*

Aim

To be able to modify clipart to get the image you want.

Resources

Computers with clipart software.

Activity

- ⊛ In any application, find a piece of clipart that shows a person.

- ⊛ Demonstrate to the class 'ungrouping' and changing the colours.

- ⊛ Ask the students to do the same, changing the clipart to look like themselves.

Differentiation

⊛ ⇓ Use a simple piece of clipart with only a few colours to change.

Cutting and copying

Objective covered
E5c *Use ICT to draft and refine a presentation, including importing and exporting data and information in appropriate formats.*

Aim
To understand what a clipboard is on a computer and how it works.

Resources
Five copies of an image.

Activity

⊛ Ask for four volunteers. Explain to volunteer 1 that they are the 'computer clipboard' and they can only hold one piece of information at a time. Tell volunteer 2 that they are the 'original document' and give them five copies of an image. Tell volunteers 3 and 4 that they are 'new documents'.

⊛ Tell the class that you are going to copy the picture from the original document. Go to volunteer 2 and collect all but one image and give them to volunteer 1. Explain that the image has been copied to the 'computer clipboard'.

⊛ Then explain that you are going to paste the image into two new documents. Give volunteers 3 and 4 a copy of the image each from volunteer 1.

⊛ Repeat the process for cutting, taking all the copies of the images from volunteer 2.

Differentiation

⊛ ⬇ Use an actual clipboard and write the steps you have taken on the board.

Picture perfect

Objective covered

E5c *Use ICT to draft and refine a presentation including importing and exporting data and information in appropriate formats.*

Aim

To know as many ways as possible to transfer images, graphics, photos or drawings into a presentation.

Activity

⊛ Write 'importing pictures' in the middle of the board.

⊛ Ask the students to come up with as many ways as possible of obtaining a picture and putting it in their work.

Answers

Internet (copy and paste), clipart, draw in paint or similar package, vector graphic drawings, draw on paper and scan image in, scan from a photo or book, digital camera and so on.

Differentiation

⊛ ⇑ In groups, ask the students to think about which would be the best way of importing the image for the purpose, for example high quality or low memory.

⊛ ⇓ Show examples to explain differences between different types of photos.

Can't do that!

Objective covered

E4 *Plan and design presentations and publications, showing how account has been taken of: audience expectations and needs; the ICT and media facilities available.*

Aim

To understand what must be taken into account when designing a symbol for a logo or roadsign.

Resources

Five symbols for display:

Activity

⊛ Ask the students what each symbol represents. They should explain what makes each design good for its purpose (simple, clear, bold, cheap to produce and so on).

⊛ Ask them to produce, by hand, a symbol to display in a park for 'no blading/rollerskating'.

Answers

No entry, radioactive, no smoking, traffic lights, corrosive liquid

Differentiation

⊛ ⬆ Ask the students to compare their symbols and explain which is better.

⊛ ⬆ Ask the students to think about the colours they would use and why.

⊛ ⬇ Choose an easier symbol to make, such as 'no ball games'.

Import this

Objective covered

E5a *Use a range of ICT tools to efficiently combine, refine and present information by extracting, combining and modifying relevant information for specific purposes.*

Aim

To be able to integrate text, graphics and numerical data into a DTP document.

Resources

Computers with word processor, spreadsheet, DTP software, and access to the Internet. Each computer should have a file containing word-processed files explaining the benefits of eating fruit and a spreadsheet listing favourite fruits:

Fruit	Number of people
Apple	45
Orange	32
Banana	34
Pear	10
Cherry	3
Plum	2
Peach	5

Activity

- Explain that the students are going to produce a poster promoting the eating of healthy food in a school.

- They should import the prepared files and an image from the Internet to use in their posters.

- Remind the students that the poster needs a title.

Differentiation

- ⇓ Talk the students through opening all of the packages first, explaining minimising and maximising.

Have you seen my cat?

Objective covered
E5a *Use a range of ICT tools to efficiently combine, refine and present information by extracting, combining and modifying relevant information for specific purposes.*

Aim
To know how to modify a poster to increase its impact.

Resources
Poster similar to the one below, either on a board or worksheet.

LOST CAT
IF FOUND
RING
01962 555555

Activity
⊛ Ask the students to list five ways in which they could improve the poster to make it look better.

Answers
Include a photo of the cat, border, clipart, text frames, description, colour and size of writing, size of poster.

Differentiation
⊛ ⇑ Ask the students to design a better poster by hand.

Lovely layout

Objective covered

E5b *Use a range of ICT tools efficiently to combine, refine and present information by structuring a publication or presentation (e.g. using document styles, templates, time lines in sound and video editing, navigational structures in web media).*

Aim

To understand the importance of structuring or laying out a page for maximum effect.

Resources

Computers with DTP software and a newsletter prepared with all the information in boxes around the outside of the page.

Activity

⊛ Tell the students to open the publication from a shared area. Ask them to move the boxes onto the page to make it look as good as possible.

⊛ They should then compare their page to someone else's and list the good points of each.

Differentiation

⊛ ⬆ Ask the students to lay out the page in two different ways and choose the better way, with reasons.

⊛ ⬇ This can be attempted as a paper exercise, fitting cut-out boxes onto a piece of paper.

Framing phrases

Objective covered

E5b *Use a range of ICT tools efficiently to combine, refine and present information by structuring a publication or presentation (e.g. using document styles, templates, time lines in sound and video editing, navigational structures in web media).*

Aim

To know the technical terms to describe the layout of the front page of a newspaper.

Activity

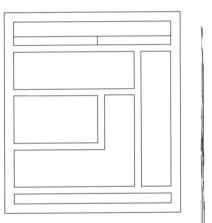

- ⊛ Either draw the template shown on the board and ask the students to copy it, or hand it out as a worksheet.

- ⊛ List the following parts of a front page of a newspaper on the board: title, headline, main article, leader, contents, second story, image.

- ⊛ Ask the students to match each label with the correct frame.

- ⊛ Explain what each of the labels means. For example, the leader is advertising an article inside the newspaper.

Answers

There is no real right and wrong, but the usual layout would be title at the top, leader below, headline below, then image and main article with second story at the side and contents at the bottom.

Differentiation

- ⊛ ⇓ Give a second worksheet with the labels written in correctly shaped boxes.

Copycat

Objective covered

E3 *Use a wide range of ICT independently and efficiently to combine, refine, interpret and present information by: structuring, refining and synthesising information from a range of sources; selecting and using software effectively, justifying the choices made.*

Aim

To know how to copy and paste information to produce a newspaper page.

Resources

Newspapers.
Computers with DTP software and Internet access.

Activity

⊛ Show the students a page from a newspaper.

⊛ Ask them to produce a similar page using information from www.bbc.co.uk. They are not allowed to type anything themselves – they can only copy and paste.

Differentiation

⊛ ⇓ Explain exactly how to get to a suitable web page and tell the students what information to copy.

Identifying icons

Objective covered

E3b *Use a wide range of ICT independently and efficiently to combine, refine, interpret and present information by selecting and using software effectively, justifying the choices made.*

Aim

To know what the standard buttons in computer applications do and when to use them.

Resources

The following table photocopied and cut up as cards.

	New	Creates a new file
	Open	Opens an existing file
	Save	Saves the file
	Print	Prints the file
	Print Preview	Shows what will be printed
	Cut	Copies selection onto clipboard then deletes it
	Copy	Copies selection onto clipboard and keeps it
	Paste	Imports what is on the clipboard onto page
	Format Painter	Copies the style of the text
	Undo	Undoes the last action

Activity

- Ask the students to get into pairs. Hand out a set of cards to each pair.
- Ask the pairs to match each icon to its name and function.

Differentiation

- ⇑ Only give the first two columns and ask the students to write the function.

I am not a number

Objective covered
E6 *Use e-mail securely and efficiently for short messages and supporting material.*

Aim
To be able to use e-mail.

Resources
Computers with e-mail capability.
You will need to have set up numbered e-mail addresses, for example 1@school.co.uk up to 30@school.co.uk.

Activity
- Allocate each student a number and ask them to match up two people with their numbers by asking questions about hobbies, interests, descriptions and so on. They are not allowed to ask names.

- Beware – this could take some time without good management!

Differentiation
- ⇩ Simply have a competition to see who can send five e-mails and get replies fastest.

Safety is the key

Objective covered

E7 *Know how to protect personal details and why this is important.*

Aim

To know ways to keep information safe on a computer system.

Activity

- ⊛ Explain to the students that it is important that information is kept secure.

- ⊛ Ask the students to think of ways to keep information secure. They should produce a list.

- ⊛ Go through students' ideas. List them on the board by categorising them into physical security (alarms, locks and so on) or virtual security (passwords, usernames and so on).

Differentiation

- ⊛ ⇧ Ask the students to categorise the information.

- ⊛ ⇩ Give examples to get the students started.

Can you guess what it is yet?

Objective covered

E6 *Understand some of the technical issues involved in efficient electronic communications (e.g. speed and bandwidth, size and type of file, features of different browsers and mail software).*

Aim

To know what file extensions are used by different applications.

Resources

Cut out the following table to make a set of cards for each pair:

.doc	Word
.xls	Excel
.pub	Publisher
.html	Internet Explorer
.bmp	Paint
.mdb	Access
.ppt	PowerPoint

Activity

⊛ Tell the students to get into pairs.

⊛ Ask each pair to match the file extension to the program that uses it.

Differentiation

⊛ ⇩ Allow the students to use a computer to help them.

Does size matter?

Objective covered

E6 *Understand some of the technical issues involved in efficient electronic communications (e.g. speed and bandwidth, size and type of file, features of different browsers and mail software).*

Aim

To understand that different files have different sizes and why this is important.

Resources

Full lever arch file and a smaller file. A page drawn on the board similar to this one:

SKIING
A great activity for all the family. This sport is very important to many people.

Activity

- ✹ Explain that computer files can be different sizes in the same way that physical files can. Show the students a full lever arch file and a smaller file.

- ✹ Explain that within a computer file, different parts take up different amounts of memory, for example an image takes up a lot more memory than text.

- ✹ Get the students to look at the page on the board. Ask them why they should do the title and text before the picture.

- ✹ Prompt them to say that if you do the picture first, the computer needs to load this regularly, which takes longer than loading text.

Differentiation

- ✹ ⇑ Ask the students to think about the order in which Internet pages load. Ask them why they think this is (most memory-intensive last).

Let's go nationwide!

Objective covered

E7 *Use ICT effectively to adapt material for publication to wider or remote audiences (e.g. as web articles or sites).*

Aim

To be able to modify a poster for use with a wider audience.

Resources

An advert for a local shop similar to this one:

Alton Bakehouse

Fresh bread daily at 1a High Street

Activity

⊛ Explain that the shop has gone nationwide and needs to update the advert.

⊛ Ask the students to redesign the advert by hand, explaining the changes.

⊛ Prompt them to think about name, not to use very specific photos, to remove location, remove prices as some areas are generally more expensive, improve the quality, use more colours.

Differentiation

⊛ ⇑ Ask the students to attempt the task on a computer.

⊛ ⇓ Only list the things that need changing.

⊛ ⇓ Show the second poster for the nationwide shop and compare it with the local one.

Low on memory

Objective covered

E4 *Apply knowledge of the technical issues involved to communicate information efficiently (e.g. choose suitable file types to speed up transfer, use mail lists to speed up communication, use website tagging and hyperlinks to speed up searching).*

Aim

To know that different types of files can perform the same function but have different attributes.

Resources

Computers with graphics package.

Activity

- ⊛ Save the same picture, the same size, as a bitmap and a jpeg file in a shared area.

- ⊛ Ask the students to open each file, compare the pictures and note the memory taken up by the file.

- ⊛ Explain that while it is easier to edit a bitmap, a jpeg takes up a lot less space.

- ⊛ Explain to the students that a wav file is a normal sound file but an mp3 is compressed by ignoring irrelevant information. For example, to go from note A to G, an mp3 assumes you will go through BCDEF.

Differentiation

- ⊛ ⇓ Look at the different file sizes and decide which type of file is better quality and which is best for transferring between computers.

Open to all?

Objective covered

E5 *Understand the advantages, dangers and moral issues in using ICT to manipulate and present information to large unknown audiences (e.g. issues of ownership, quality control, exclusion, impact on particular communities).*

Aim

To understand that targeting certain media will exclude percentages of the population.

Resources

A class set of cards similar to those shown below with symbols to represent telephone, e-mail, texting and post.

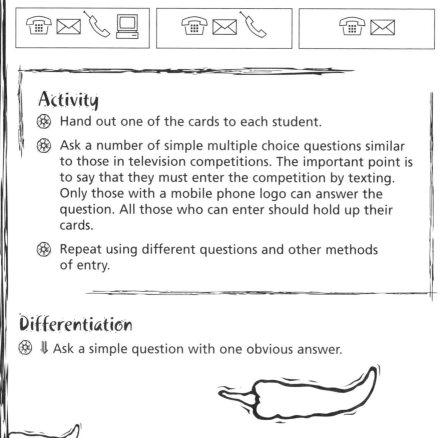

Activity

⊛ Hand out one of the cards to each student.

⊛ Ask a number of simple multiple choice questions similar to those in television competitions. The important point is to say that they must enter the competition by texting. Only those with a mobile phone logo can answer the question. All those who can enter should hold up their cards.

⊛ Repeat using different questions and other methods of entry.

Differentiation

⊛ ⇓ Ask a simple question with one obvious answer.

I wouldn't show that

Objective covered

E5 *Understand the advantages, dangers and moral issues in using ICT to manipulate and present information to large unknown audiences (e.g. issues of ownership, quality control, exclusion, impact on particular communities).*

Aim

To understand that there are limitations when creating a public website.

Activity

⚙ Use a spider diagram to brainstorm the issues involved in creating a school website. Ideas should include personal information, addresses, exam results, medical problems, legitimacy of notices on the guestbook, monitoring of messages and keeping up to date.

⚙ Ask the students to come up with some guidelines for teachers to consider when making a school website.

Differentiation

⚙ ⇓ Ask the students to list things that should not be available to the public on a website.

In the wrong hands

Objective covered

E5 *Understand the advantages, dangers and moral issues in using ICT to manipulate and present information to large unknown audiences (e.g. issues of ownership, quality control, exclusion, impact on particular communities).*

Aim

To understand how easy it is for information to fall into the wrong hands once published on the Internet.

Resources

Small pieces of paper.

Activity

⊛ Explain to the students that they shouldn't give out their name, address or phone number on the Internet as some people might abuse the information. It only takes one person to pass information on for it to spread worldwide.

⊛ Give each student one small piece of paper. Ask one student to write a six-figure number on their piece of paper (to represent a phone number).

⊛ Explain that you want to see how fast this information spreads. Ask the student to pass the piece of paper to another student, who copies it and passes both pieces on. The next two students copy the number and pass it on to two more each and so on.

⊛ Explain to the students that information and viruses can be passed this quickly over the Internet. Ask them to imagine how quickly a credit card number could fall into the wrong hands.

Differentiation

⊛ ⇓ Use a two-figure number.